Invasions
of the Heart

Genara Necos

Copyright © 2017 Genara Necos

The moral right of the author has been asserted.

Apart from any fair dealing for the purposes of research or private study, or criticism or review, as permitted under the Copyright, Designs and Patents Act 1988, this publication may only be reproduced, stored or transmitted, in any form or by any means, with the prior permission in writing of the publishers, or in the case of reprographic reproduction in accordance with the terms of licences issued by the Copyright Licensing Agency. Enquiries concerning reproduction outside those terms should be sent to the publishers.

Matador
9 Priory Business Park,
Wistow Road, Kibworth Beauchamp,
Leicestershire. LE8 0RX
Tel: 0116 279 2299
Email: books@troubador.co.uk
Web: www.troubador.co.uk/matador
Twitter: @matadorbooks

ISBN 978 1788033 169

British Library Cataloguing in Publication Data.
A catalogue record for this book is available from the British Library.

Typeset in 11pt Minion Pro by Troubador Publishing Ltd, Leicester, UK

Matador is an imprint of Troubador Publishing Ltd

To my sister Belkis who lives in my heart.

Foreign Affairs

What is Florence?
Orange blossoms and the Pontevechio…
At the Villa Giardino
The cypress brushed the moon-
Opulent ball falling into my hands.
Silver wolves howled,
But I had no fear
Desire was my spear.
What is Florence?
The ethereal blue bathing the chiesa
So like the blue of your eyes.
The Ospedali Degli Inocenti…

But who is innocenti?
She rose tumultuous
Out of the turquoise waters at Tonfano
Her lips parted forming an O
Opulent as the moon.

At the Villa Giardino
The wolves stopped howling.
Silenced by the sight
of black hair and white thighs drenched in Vin Santo light,
Glowing.
Silenced by your bodies
like a sunset in flames…
You see, it's the bodies one blames…

Desire, my spear
thrust at me with treacherous might….
Douse me with orange blossoms
Stroll me on the Pontevecchio…

What is Florence?
The City of dreams I had not dreamt.

The Pelican

Umber wings form the V of the conqueror
On powder blue skies
Swoop into platinum depths
Rise
More formidable than Top Guns
Who built a "Path in the Sea"
More beautiful than Tom Cruise.
He reigns
Above a glass city built with ancient blood
Above village roads where the Embera and the Kuna
Brood.
His majesty demands
For the pillaged
After La Pinta, **La Nina** & La Santa Maria…
The Resurrection of
The ravaged…

Mission in Panama, 2012

Baile En Nueva York

Dance merengue
Bronze thighs ablaze
Hibiscus flowing down
Your peach sarong
Dance
Revel in Song
Trample Soil
Soaked with memories
Of swinging and swaying
Of the sea's sapphire daze.
Dance, Dance
Hips swiveling,
Breasts swelling,
Feet stomping stems.

Turn.

Reach for the sun,
Rising over steel birds spewing black haze.
How can this be the same sun?
Now falling behind the Watchtower Clock,
This Sun
So eager to Mock
So far away from the sapphire sea
So far away from childhood.

Invasions

They said men
With eyes like river blue stones
Appeared on our island
But Luisa did not believe
In mythical beings she had never seen
She was as old as the Century
It was 1917.

From morn till twilight her job was to wash
The head laundress paid her in cash
Her hands and her body were a strong chlorite black.
Her shoulders belied her fatigue and so did her supple back.

These men with eyes like river blue stones
and weapons named
Colt and Berretta
More majestic than any escopeta
Came, as General Arias fled,
To bring order to our backwards Republica Dominicana,
So they said
Luisa listened and washed
Unafraid

The men reveled
Lost their heads,
So their Captain Knapp
Found it apt
To put <u>us</u> under Toque De Queda
"Now. Before dusk. Go to your beds!"

It was while Luisa washed
That the River soldier came
Leaking blue light from his eyes
The head laundress smiled—As she let him in--
"Luisa remember don't mix up the dyes."

He put his majestic Colt on the ground
Ah, Luisa was sad for him…
Not yet 20 and far away from home
No woman to wash for him,
And his daily dealings with Dominicanos were bound to confound

Fear and desolation bore through his pale hand
As he reached for her supple back
His eyes grew grey as the bullets in his Colt
Luisa knew it was her moment to bolt

She called the head laundress
Who ignored her distress
She sought to beseech
As he made his demand….

His weapon— of flesh-- pierced her womb –
Scathe like hot bleach.

Her cries
Drowned
In the bottomless blue of his river stone eyes.

Powder

I didn't know about Cortina and Chamonix
And Vail, where the snow glimmers like diamonds spliced into the mountain slope,
So close to the Marigold Sun.
In the Bronx, the snow covered the sidewalks;
We played just long enough to see it melt into a polish that devoured the sun
Tia burned her mother
Rafael overdosed on the roof,
Carlos and Marcelino pitched a man from that roof
Walking to PS 11, we saw men asleep while standing,
Waking, just long enough to want to doze for life-
So you ski, hah?
Tell me about powder.
About the pinnacle- the high when all you see is white,
The boys I knew,
They never said "danger," the way that you do,
Casually and, remarkably, coolly,
"the danger of leaving resort grounds to climb back country slopes, the thrill….."
On a winter night, when the moon shed so much light you could dance on the streets
I saw a man bleeding under the oak benches of the Bronx Diner; someone dragged him out
To bleed in the mud…….Snow.

The Princess in Paris

Once
We savored each strand
Of your caramel hair
At the local newsstand
People told
Pages sold
As a dark knife
Slashed at your silver spoon life
Plagued by Divorce
Motherless, widowed
Wallowing in Adultery
It was no mystery
Under the glare
You shed your silken hair
Once
We glimpsed each other
Royalty and Peasantry
In the city that glows like cathedral candles
It's my life now in shambles
Should I tell People
Of my single motherhood
My lonely poverty
Would People care?
It is so clear
In my anonymous despair
I cherish my kinky hair.

Foreign Affairs II

At the Italian Bakery in Harare
I went in search of Espresso,
And found you, a bold Ristretto,
Regal as a Zulu warrior
Fan of "Andy Brown and the Storm,"
Silent carrier of Thunder
While falling, I did not grow wings,
I landed like winter Jacarandas
Strewn on the road after so many springs
At the Italian Bakery in Harare,
Where all was sweet, and crisp as my childhood mornings,
Festive as a whirl
to La Bamba,
I went looking for Espresso, and found you,
A Dark, Delicious Swirl
Perilous as a Mamba.

Couple in the City

Aimless
As debris floating in the waters of a bankrupt city--
Its hidden gangs plotting
Its rats…
Their brown mossy coats
Flying under bare branches--
You and I face each other
Wishing we could turn back the gnarled fingers
Of time slamming the city gates in our faces
Doubts linger….
Will we ever sate this hunger…
But I take your marred hand in mine
We walk along the city's edge--
Sharp as the cold searing our center--
Broken
Homeless
Going
Going
Together……

A Bridge Grows in Brooklyn

I leave "Baked in Brooklyn."

To cross under
A buttery sun-
Into the Greenwood Cemetery
To me, this is fun

Surrounded by Death
My hands full of bread
Finches yellow as glory fly overhead
A golden bridge
To a child laid to rest in innocence in 1888
Not a second too late
A Bridge to Basquiat laid to rest in penance in 1988
Why couldn't he wait?

Basquiat speaks of Lawrence
So different from him and from his life on the run
Of how with the reverence
his mind spun and spun
Of terrors at night
Of peace from a needle with liquid light

A cardinal sings his song of Faith
His feathers like bloody petals on a stem

I hear Bernstein Now….
"It's us versus them,
An artist must stand
Against cruel demand
Though stricken sometimes
Through difficult climes
I feared but I fought, I opted to stay."

He doesn't speak of symphonies
Nor of West Side Stories
But of Brooklyn's bridges versus Canaletto's "flurries."
"Ah so what about Canaletto, he never crossed the Verrazano."
Basquiat with raised eyebrow
Chuckles, "no mi hermano."

And I, my heart above the city fray
On this brilliant blue day
Join Bernstein and Basquiat as we say

"I love Brooklyn."

Eating Pears

Late autumn nights
Pears glisten
Like sun tanned skin_
I bite into flesh
As sweet as ours was salty
That hottest summer day.

Morning Dream

The recess of a dream
Calls me
Like a shadow longing for a body to cast.

Depression

The black river
Like a blanket in a millennial hotel
Beckons_
Come under- It's night
In my dark embrace
Softer than a feline's fleece
You'll find all you seek--
Peace

A Return to Hope

Memories assaulted me
Held me behind locked yesterdays
That exploded on a windless
Evening.

Memories, I said
Where are you taking me?
Back to the Avenue of yourself
The one with the interior courtyard
The deep cool garden
The fountain
Where you took in the sunset
With that thin sweet neighbor
Who poured coffee
And stirred it,
Just for you….
On those days
When the mornings started
Full of promises
Of tomorrow.

At Trinity During Spiritual Journaling, September 29, 2016

Lightning Source UK Ltd.
Milton Keynes UK
UKHW02f1046110618
324036UK00006B/194/P

Lightning Source UK Ltd.
Milton Keynes UK
UKHW02f1046110618
324036UK00006B/194/P